This book is dedicated to all who cherish

America's history as a vast heritage of people and events — some

heroic, some inglorious, but all part of America's epic struggle

to come of age — and to all who know that understanding

the past is essential to dealing with the present.

GETTYSBURG
THE STORY BEHIND THE SCENERY®

by William C. Davis
Photography by David Muench

William C. "Jack" Davis served for 13 years as editor of the magazine *Civil War Times Illustrated,* and is the author of 15 books on that war, including the six-volume photographic history *Image of War.* Jack has twice been nominated for the Pulitzer Prize. He lives just 25 miles from the Gettysburg battlefield in an old country inn briefly occupied by Union troops during the campaign.

David Muench, one of the country's foremost landscape photographers, brings to these pages keen sensitivity and an artist's instinct for the blending of color, form, and mood. His rapport with the natural world enables him to photograph brilliantly both the majestic battleground and the rolling countryside of Gettysburg.

Gettysburg National Military Park, *located in southeastern Pennsylvania, was established in 1895 to preserve the site of the great Civil War battle fought July 1-3, 1863.*

Front cover: Statue of General George G. Meade, Cemetery Ridge. Inside front cover: Virginia Monument, Robert E. Lee. Page 1: Sunrise at High Water Mark. Pages 2/3: The Copse of Trees on Cemetery Ridge.

Book design by K. C. DenDooven

Fourth Printing, 1993

GETTYSBURG: THE STORY BEHIND THE SCENERY. © 1983 KC PUBLICATIONS, INC.
LC 83-80606. ISBN 0-916122-89-1.

For those who come to Gettysburg there is a journey back in time to a battleground where armies converged and men gallantly rose to do battle. Had it not been for those three July days when Federals and Confederates fought and died in its streets and surrounding fields and hills, this quiet Pennsylvania town would be as little known today as it was before they clashed more than a century ago.

Over the centuries warring armies have tramped most of the globe, meeting for a few brief moments of bloodletting before continuing their odyssey. In some of those conflicts the places where they met to do battle were already scenes of note. Quebec. Berlin. Moscow. New Orleans. Manila. In large measure the Civil War was different. It stands unique among conflicts for the number of simple, humble places that it immortalized.

To be sure, the armies of Blue and Gray met at Nashville, fought for Richmond, even skirmished outside Washington. But the war was won and lost on other battlefields—sites not likely to be remembered otherwise. Shiloh. Manassas. Westport. Antietam. The Wilderness. Some of these locations did not even appear on maps of that era. Yet so important did they become when the armies came together that their names are emblazoned forever on the national consciousness. Standing above all the others is Gettysburg.

Had it not been for those three days that Federals and Confederates fought and died in its streets and in the surrounding fields and hills, this quiet south central Pennsylvania town would be as little known today as it was more than a century ago before the armies clashed. Gettysburg was a farming community, a rural county seat of little note. The town boasted three newspapers. From nearby Hanover the Western Maryland Railway connected Gettysburg with Baltimore. Pennsylvania College, now Gettysburg College, and a Lutheran seminary held classes here.

West and south of town there are two parallel ridges separated by three quarters of a mile or more. Immediately south of Gettysburg lies Cemetery Hill, so named to memorialize nearby Evergreen Cemetery. Cemetery Ridge extends south from the hill for nearly two miles before it terminates in two knoblike hills: Little Round Top, and beyond it, Big Round Top. Three quarters of a mile west of the Round Tops, Seminary Ridge rises and runs north, parallel to Cemetery Ridge, for nearly five miles and ends northwest of Gettysburg at Oak Hill and Oak Ridge. Those long lines of hills and ridges helped make Gettysburg a perfect place for a nineteenth-century battle.

Preceding pages: The Copse of Trees on Cemetery Ridge at Gettysburg.

The armies were en route to Gettysburg long before they knew what terrain they would encounter. Converging roads led them here, making some sort of confrontation almost inevitable. Robert E. Lee had invaded the North in June 1863, marching from Virginia through Maryland into Pennsylvania, hoping to take Harrisburg, the latter's state capital; disrupt Federal railroads; and gather sorely needed supplies from the enemy's "bread basket." As Lee speedily advanced, existing roads were taking him toward Gettys-

Gettysburg as seen from Oak Ridge.

Battle at Gettysburg

burg. General George G. Meade was the officer who had just assumed command of the Union Army of the Potomac on June 28, 1863. If he was to stop Lee, he had no choice but to use other roads in the area to convey him and his troops here also. If Gettysburg was of no importance otherwise, it was an intersection of no less than ten thoroughfares. All roads, it seemed, led to Gettysburg.

Here on June 30 began their encounter, and for three days they tore and ripped at each other. The following day, July 1, Major General Henry Heth was sent with his entire division, with orders to clear Brigadier General John Buford's cavalry out of Gettysburg. The Confederates came upon the cavalry of Brigadier General John Buford. Northwest of town the heavily outnumbered Yankees courageously attempted to hold back the gray tide. Union commander, General John Buford, determined to hold the vital crossroads town, initiated a valiant defense while waiting for reinforcements to arrive.

General John Reynolds's I Corps and General

Over the boulder-strewn slopes of Little Round Top, thousands battled on July 2, 1863. Upon this summit, with its wide vista of the entire length of Meade's line, lay the key to the battlefield. From this crest fire-breathing cannon might control the entire southern half of the field.

Oliver O. Howard's XI Corps soon arrived, but so had substantially greater numbers of Confederates. In and around Herbst's (or Reynolds's) Woods, Oak Hill, and the northern end of Seminary Ridge the battle raged. Reynolds fell from his horse, dead on his native Pennsylvania soil. Action seesawed back and forth, with heavy losses to both sides. Late in the afternoon the Southerners steadily pushed back their foes. Lee had begun the fighting with more of his army closer to Gettysburg than Meade's. By day's end the Federals had been forced back through and beyond the town to a tenuous line on Cemetery Hill and Cemetery Ridge. Lee seemed to have all the odds—it seemed that another victory for the Army of Northern Virginia awaited only the dawn.

All night long, after the fighting died away, thousands of men in blue and gray rushed toward the battlefield. By the next morning, July 2, both armies were committed to a major battle here that neither commander had really wanted. Meade spread his army along the ridge leading south from town and east from Cemetery Hill to Culp's Hill and beyond. He was fearful that Lee would attack on the right flank of his line, and cut off his communications and possible line of retreat to Baltimore. Thus Meade focused much of his attention on this part of his line. Below Cemetery Ridge lay two rocky and partially wooded knobs: Little Round Top, and south of it, the almost impassable Big Round Top. They had a commanding view of the Union line. If Confederates should seize Little Round Top and emplace artillery, Meade's entire line would be vulnerable.

Lee's plan was to attack northward along Emmitsburg Road and go up along Meade's left flank. He sent General James Longstreet, commanding his I Corps, with orders to attack. As it happened, General Daniel Sickles, one of Meade's corps commanders, had exceeded his orders and placed his III Corps not at the southern end of Cemetery Ridge as ordered, but far in advance of it—through a wheat field and a peach orchard, where he lay fully exposed to Longstreet's attack. When the blow fell, Sickles's corps was decimated. A Confederate shell nearly blew off one of the general's legs. It was amputated later that day. After a long seesaw battle his corps gave up its position with terrible losses, and Longstreet's men swarmed through the orchard and wheat field, past a rock outcrop called the Devil's Den, and toward the slopes of Little Round Top.

Federals barely beat the Rebels to the summit. Indeed, that afternoon one of Longstreet's divisions, led by General John B. Hood, had almost walked up the slope unopposed. General Gouverneur K. Warren, Meade's principal engineer, seems to have recognized before anyone else the threat that a Conferate-held Little Round Top would pose. On his own authority Warren commandeered troops and placed cannon on the summit. In response to Warren's urgent plea for reinforcements, General George Sykes, V Corps commander, issued an order dispatching a brigade to Little Round Top. Colonel Strong Vincent intercepted Sykes's order, and soon his brigade was rushing up the northern slope and over the crest. Hood's Confederates were actually partway up the slope when the Federals at last amassed sufficient strength to defend the hill. In the bitter

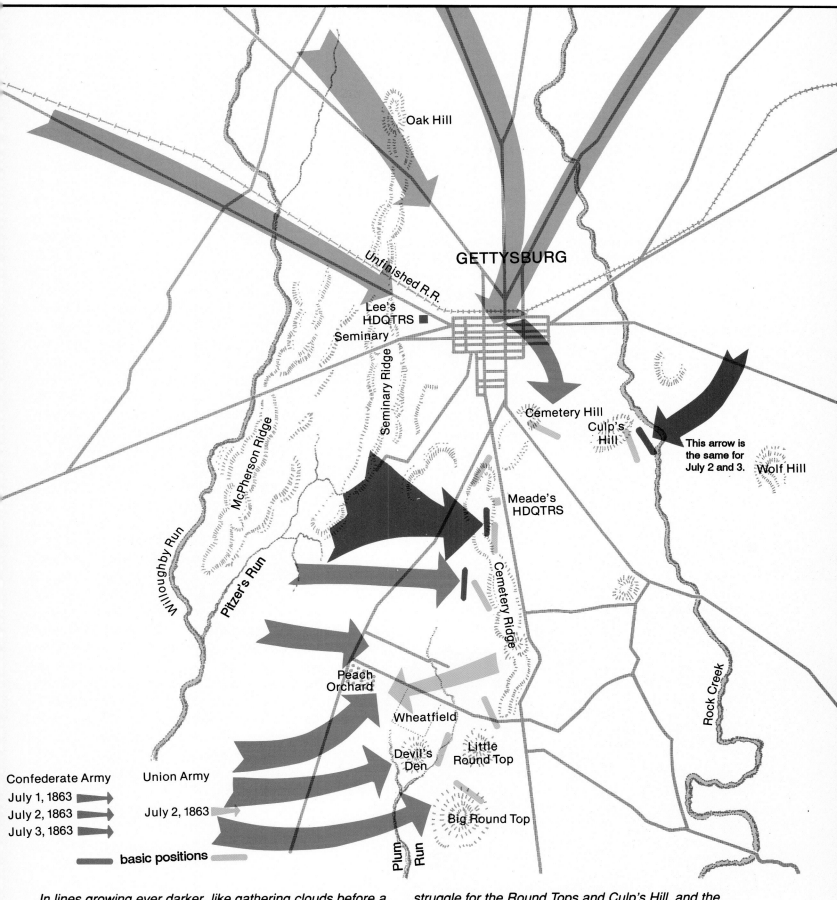

Oak Hill

GETTYSBURG

Unfinished R.R.

Lee's
HDQTRS

Seminary

Seminary Ridge

McPherson Ridge

Willoughby Run

Pitzer's Run

Cemetery Hill
Culp's
Hill

This arrow is
the same for
July 2 and 3.

Wolf Hill

Meade's
HDQTRS

Cemetery Ridge

Rock Creek

Peach
Orchard

Wheatfield

Devil's
Den

Little
Round Top

Big Round Top

Plum Run

Confederate Army
July 1, 1863
July 2, 1863
July 3, 1863

Union Army

July 2, 1863

basic positions

In lines growing ever darker, like gathering clouds before a raging storm, arrows tell the story of three days at Gettysburg. That first day, July 1, Confederates drove their out-numbered foe off Oak Hill and Seminary Ridge, off the plains north of Gettysburg and back through town. On the next day the great assaults at either end of the line, the struggle for the Round Tops and Culp's Hill, and the encounter in the Wheatfield and Peach Orchard took place. At last, on that fatal July 3, came the final charge on Cemetery Ridge. On the morning of July 3 there was almost seven hours fierce fighting on Culp's Hill.

fighting that followed, the brave Vincent fell mortally wounded among the boulders of Little Round Top. His foresight and that of General Warren, coupled with the desperate fighting of V Corps, had perhaps prevented a Union disaster.

On that day disaster had almost struck Meade at the other end of his line as well, where his position curved eastward from Cemetery Hill to Culp's Hill. Confederates led by General Richard S. Ewell had been tardy in launching the attack Lee wanted. Not until after 6:00 that evening did the real assault start. By that time Meade had so weakened this part of his line by pulling out troops to reinforce his left, that most of Culp's Hill was defended by but a single brigade. Though attacked by almost an entire enemy division, those stalwart Yankees held the hill until after nightfall on the second day. Had Lee been successful here and in a nearby attack on the northern end of Cemetery Hill, he would have had a clear road to the Federal rear. If Hood had then taken Little Round Top, the entire Northern army would have been caught between two pincers, with no line of retreat and under threat of enemy artillery from that vital summit.

Great battles made hallowed spots of humble places; none more so than the little house in which General Meade made his headquarters. Here on July 2 he made the fateful decision to stand and fight another day.

Meade might very possibly have had his entire army destroyed or surrendered.

For two days the battle had been precarious for the Federals. That night, July 2, Meade met with his commanders in his headquarters, a tiny house that is still standing, just behind the crest of Cemetery Hill. Should he stay and fight, or had the army already endured too many near misses? Unanimously, his generals opted to stand their ground. Meade stood with them.

On the two previous days Lee had tried to attack both Meade's left and right flanks. By noon on July 3 there was only one last alternative: the center—the line on Cemetery Ridge. Lee's most trusted general, Longstreet, objected to such an assault, but Lee believed it could succeed. At 1:00 P.M. Lee opened a massive artillery bombardment. For over an hour Meade answered, then stopped to save ammunition. Lee did not know that much of his fire had passed harmlessly over the Federal line. When Meade held his return fire, it appeared that the Yankee guns had been silenced. This, then, was the moment to attack.

Half an hour later a reluctant Longstreet sent forward the divisions of James J. Pettigrew, Isaac Trimble, and the man whose name would cling forever to the ensuing assault: George E. Pickett. About 12,000 Confederates marched in ranks down Seminary Ridge's slopes and across more than half a mile of open ground toward Cemetery Ridge. It was one of the grandest frontal assaults the South would ever launch, but it was doomed from the start. The Confederates first encountered artillery fire, then the bullets of Yankee infantrymen. In the end, only a few hundred Rebels actually reached the Union line. In some places fighting was hand to hand. Federal reinforcements rushed to the line. A handful of Southerners actually penetrated Meade's defenses; the rest were driven back or were consumed in the inferno of Federal fire. Rallying as best they could, the Rebels staggered back to a hard-pressed Lee. That ended the offensive.

The armies were exhausted. For a day they sat and faced each other without fighting, Lee too defiant to admit his defeat, Meade too tired to follow up his victory. Two armies totaling more than 160,000 men had battled each other. Now nearly 50,000 of them were casualties. Cessation of hostilities signaled an end to Lee's invasion, an end some would later say, to the Confederacy itself. It marked one of several turning points in the war. Yet it was a beginning as well. Never again would Gettysburg be a place unknown in

the United States. For in three sweltering July days in 1863 it had risen above itself and above all other battles of that war to signify the best and worst in warfare. It gripped the attention of men and women everywhere. North and South were never quite the same. After this struggle, neither was Gettysburg.

The ground around Gettysburg is hard and rocky. Located at the base of Culp's Hill, Spangler's Spring is a natural place for defense, with every boulder a fortification. Soldiers on both sides made good use of what the ground afforded them for protection.

AFTERMATH

On July 4, 1863, and in the days immediately following the conflict, Gettysburg was a town with a substantial problem. The living population was outnumbered by that of the dead. Over 6,000 bodies lay in the fields and hills, crumpled among the boulders on Little Round Top, or wedged in the rock crevices of Devil's Den. Immediate action was necessary. The hot July sun caused the bodies to decompose rapidly. Soldiers and civilian volunteers hastily dug thousands of shallow graves, often burying men where they had fallen or placing them in long rows of shallow trenches. In doing so, they did not take into account the elements. When it came, rain quickly washed away the scanty layers of soil above the interred dead, and what the showers did not disturb, local farmers did. These were fields where more than bodies had to be sown. Later, as farmers plowed their land in preparation for crops, they uncovered more bodies.

Shortly after the battle, Governor Andrew Curtin came from Harrisburg to assess the damage suffered by Gettysburg property owners. At the time of his visit the graves appeared to be in good order. In later weeks, however, summer rains revealed inadequate graves, and the dead became exposed. There was a clear danger that the names of the slain, roughly inscribed in pencil on wooden headboards, would soon be lost. Curtin was acquainted with a local Gettysburg attorney, David Wills. Acting for the Commonwealth of Pennsylvania, the governor empowered Wills to locate and buy a suitable parcel of ground where Union dead could be reinterred in an appropriate and permanent manner. There was less interest in the Confederate dead. There was still a war on.

Wills immediately focused upon the eastern portion of Cemetery Hill, which was adjacent to the existing Evergreen Cemetery. But another Gettysburg attorney had beaten him to it. David McConaughy, president of the Evergreen Cemetery Association, was the person charged with somehow saving that insolvent enterprise. He envisioned purchasing land surrounding the existing cemetery, then incorporating into this area the planned soldiers' burial ground. Making the two into one would enhance his enterprise, put Evergreen in the black, and in the process, produce a much more attractive cemetery and preserve a notable part of the Union defenses.

Governor Curtin would have none of it. He was determined that the soldiers' cemetery remain separate. Faced with no alternative, Mc-

Conaughy agreed to sell the Cemetery Hill land to Evergreen Cemetery, which would sell it to the state of Pennsylvania for the new Soldiers' National Cemetery. However, McConaughy had more in mind than just graveyards. He, like many others, recognized that something extraordinary, even in wartime, had occurred at Gettysburg—something that deserved to be commemorated. There was no National Park Service then, no concerted national movement to mark or preserve places of scenic or historic value. But that did not mean that Americans felt no concern. On the contrary, they possessed a surprising devotion to their own past, a sense of their place in the

world, and a recognition of the psychological and educational benefits of preserving those places important in their country's local and national history.

Forty years before the Battle of Gettysburg, in 1823, the Bunker Hill Memorial Association had been formed to obtain and erect a giant obelisk near the site of that Revolutionary War battle. Just a decade before Lee and Meade had clashed, the Mount Vernon Ladies Association had organized to preserve George Washington's home on the banks of the Potomac River. There were annual celebrations at Tippecanoe and on Lexington Green. Why not at Gettysburg?

There was little mist or fog on those hot July days, but the smoke from thousands of guns covered the battlefield and often obscured friend from foe and friend from friend.
Atop Cemetery Hill, from behind one of the miles of stone walls on the battlefield, monuments now stand enshrouded in the fog, just as more than a century ago the men they commemorate stood there engulfed in the clouds of battle.

National Cemetery at Gettysburg

David McConaughy believed that the battle waged at Gettysburg was just as deserving of memorialization as predecessors like Bunker Hill. To his way of thinking, the Gettysburg engagement had ended a dire threat to the North, might have saved Washington from attack, and perhaps had even preserved the Union. On August 14, 1863, the same day on which General Meade was having his first conference with President Lincoln and his cabinet to detail the Gettysburg campaign, McConaughy made a proposal to a number of Gettysburg's more prominent businessmen and civic leaders. "There could be no more fitting and expressive memorial of the heroic valor and signal triumph of our army," he told them, "than the battle-field itself." He proposed that they acquire and preserve as much as possible of the field, complete with its defenses "preserved and perpetuated in the exact form and condition they presented during the battle."

It must have been very gratifying indeed when McConaughy learned that the townspeople agreed with him. His was "a happy and patriotic conception," they affirmed. Gettysburg and what had taken place there were an example well suited "to perpetuate the great principles of human liberty and just government in the minds of our descendants, and of all men who in all time shall visit them." Already residents were envisioning a place to which future generations of visitors would journey to see, learn, and appreciate. Thus, they had committed themselves to giving their battlefield "commemoration to the latest posterity in every way in which such triumphs can be consecrated."

In September 1863 citizens of Gettysburg began organizing themselves, but the enterprising McConaughy was far ahead of them. He had already begun acquiring Culp's Hill, a portion of Big Round Top, and the slopes of Little Round Top. He had also purchased the eastern slope of Cemetery Hill and Stevens' Knoll between Culp's and Cemetery hills. The lawyer had bought the land with his own funds, expecting to be reimbursed by the state when the property became an official memorial. He would have to wait a few years, however, for as the fall of 1863 approached, more pressing concerns faced Gettysburg.

Once Wills had acquired the Cemetery Hill property from Evergreen Cemetery, the U.S. Department of Agriculture provided the services of prominent landscape architect William Saunders. Saunders was to design a plan for the 17 acres of ground that were to hold the bodies of some 3,500 Union dead. His proposal called for separate lots to hold only each state's native sons, each lot sized in proportion to the number of dead. Upon solicitation from Wills and Curtin, Northern states each made proportionate financial contributions to help advance the project. Saunders produced a plan that called for a central monument to the dead, with graves extending out from it in semicircular rows. The plan was submitted to a board of commissioners, composed of men from several Union states, who immediately approved it. The board proposed that a formal dedication be arranged. Thus it was that on November 19, 1863, President Abraham Lincoln and Massachusetts orator Edward Everett came to speak at the ceremony.

The somber task of reinterment was under way when the solemn observance began. From the podium Everett spoke for two hours in a florid oration typical of that era. Lincoln, on the other hand, spoke for about two minutes, yet captured to perfection the spirit of the commemoration. Here they were, said he, gathered on a great battlefield. "We have come to dedicate a portion of that field, as a final resting place for those who here gave their lives." The world, he proclaimed, "can never forget what they did here."

The New York State Monument is prominent in the National Cemetery.

Address delivered at the dedication of the Cemetery at Gettysburg.

Four score and seven years ago our fathers brought forth on this continent, a new nation, conceived in Liberty, and dedicated to the proposition that all men are created equal.

Now we are engaged in a great civil war, testing whether that nation, or any nation so conceived and so dedicated, can long endure. We are met on a great battle-field of that war. We have come to dedicate a portion of that field, as a final resting place for those who here gave their lives that that nation might live. It is altogether fitting and proper that we should do this.

But, in a larger sense, we can not dedi-

14

cate— we can not consecrate— we can not
hallow— this ground. The brave men, living and dead, who struggled here, have consecrated it, far above our poor power to add
or detract. The world will little note, nor
long remember what we say here, but it can
never forget what they did here. It is for us
the living, rather, to be dedicated here to
the unfinished work which they who fought here have thus far so nobly advanced.
It is rather for us to be here dedicated to
the great task remaining before us— that
from these honored dead we take increased
devotion to that cause for which they gave
the last full measure of devotion— that
we here highly resolve that these dead shall
not have died in vain— that this nation,
under God, shall have a new birth of free-
dom— and that government of the people,

by the people, for the people, shall not perish from the earth.

Abraham Lincoln.

November 19, 1863.

In a few simple words of such power and meaning that they have become a part of every American's creed, Abraham Lincoln called upon his country to rise above itself. This copy, one of five by his own hand, is now in the White House, where the spirit and voice of Lincoln still linger.

It took several months to complete the work of reburying the dead. Fortunately, many of the fragile headboards with their precious identifications lasted long enough for the information to be transferred to cemetery records. Nevertheless, there were 1,664 nameless bodies, their identities known only to the Almighty. As the war continued, so did work on the Soldiers' National Cemetery. The grounds were beautified and enclosed within a stone wall. On the Fourth of July of 1865 the cornerstone of the Soldiers' National Monument was laid. Four years later the monument, a giant shaft of granite topped with a marble statue depicting the "Spirit of Liberty," was completed and dedicated.

CHANGES

By the time the Soldiers' National Monument had been dedicated in 1869, there were changes in the offing for the cemetery. Management by such a large board of commissioners had proved awkward, and in 1868 it was proposed that Pennsylvania transfer responsibility to the federal government. On May 1, 1872, formal title to the Soldiers' National Cemetery passed to the U.S. War Department, which was even then acquiring and establishing other Civil War soldiers' cemeteries. The National Cemetery remained in the hands of the War Department for another 61 years. In 1933 its management was turned over to the National Park Service.

Years earlier, McConaughy's proposal had also resulted in the organization of the Gettysburg Battlefield Memorial Association (GBMA). On April 30, 1864, the Commonwealth of Pennsylvania formally chartered the group, specifying that it consist of a president and a board of 21 directors elected annually by members of the association. Membership was extended to anyone who made a ten-dollar donation. In addition to a vote, the member was also entitled to an engraved certificate.

According to its charter, the purpose of the GBMA was to "hold, and preserve, the battlegrounds of Gettysburg," and with them, "such memorial structures as a generous and patriotic people may aid to erect, to commemorate the heroic deeds, the struggles, and the triumphs of their brave defenders." The charter and a supplemental act of the state legislature in 1866 empowered the association to buy land, lay out roads and avenues, build memorial structures, and even condemn land in order to acquire it. At the same time the GBMA's property was declared forever exempt from taxes. The farseeing McConaughy became the association's legal counsel,

Only at Gettysburg does there stand a memorial to a single speech. The Lincoln Address Memorial recalls from amidst the horrors of war the most enduring of appeals for peace.

and to him was entrusted the task of raising contributions from the various Northern states. Governors of those states whose legislatures made donations automatically became members of the board of directors.

But the work did not proceed as McConaughy had envisioned. In 1864 the Pennsylvania state legislature provided $4,000 for the Gettysburg Battlefield Memorial Association. However, contributions and memberships to the GBMA were not forthcoming. With the nation still recovering from the conflict, even the more affluent Northern states seemed reluctant at first to spend money on recalling a war that most wanted only to forget. Not surprisingly, it remained for the veterans themselves to get the association moving.

In 1878 the Pennsylvania division of the Union veterans' organization, the Grand Army of the Republic, held the first reunion at Gettysburg. Before that time the only substantial memorials on the field were the Soldiers' National Monument and a statue of General John F. Reynolds, both in the National Cemetery. During this reunion a marble marker was erected that would designate the site where Colonel Strong Vincent had been mortally wounded in defending Little Round Top. Soon thereafter a marker to another fallen Pennsylvanian went up, and in 1879 the veterans of the 2d Massachusetts Infantry purchased and erected the first regimental monument on the battlefield.

Realizing what they could achieve at Gettys-

burg, GAR posts all across the United States initiated an active campaign to urge veterans to buy memberships in the GBMA. With memberships came votes, and by 1880 the GAR held enough ballots to gain control of the association's board of directors. In addition to individual donations, scores of GAR posts made group contributions. Within a very few years the association and the battlefield memorial experienced a burst of growth and prosperity.

By 1888, the twenty-fifth anniversary of the battle, the association held title to almost 500 acres of ground. This acreage included the grove on McPherson's Ridge where General Reynolds had been killed, portions of both Round Tops, the Wheatfield, Devil's Den, Culp's Hill, the eastern portion of Cemetery Hill, and much of the line along Cemetery Ridge that General Meade had occupied. Some 13 miles of driveway had been constructed along the location of the Federal lines, and a major portion of battlefield land had been safely enclosed in wire fencing. As yet there had been no effort to acquire or preserve sites connected with the Confederate role in the Battle of Gettysburg.

In 1888 and the years just preceding it, a forest of markers and monuments had sprouted all over the Gettysburg battlefield areas. There were over 200 of them when Union veterans gathered for their twenty-fifth reunion. Special markers had been placed where leading commanders had been killed or wounded. Several

This portion of rock wall was not built by soldiers but was part of Abraham Spangler's farm boundary. The wall was used for defense. Many of the rock walls erected for the battle have remained standing — others have been rebuilt.

miles away from Gettysburg, at the scene of the oft-forgotten cavalry fighting that had also been part of the engagement, a memorial column commemorating the role of Union horsemen had been dedicated.

A BATTLEFIELD TAKES SHAPE

The Gettysburg battlefield continued to expand in the next few years. More land was acquired, including some 30 acres taken by condemnation. In 1878 a wooden "observatory" was built on East Cemetery Hill, offering a view of most of the scene of the conflict. Breastworks erected during the clash had been maintained or restored. The town of Gettysburg began to enjoy a modest income from a burgeoning tourist industry. "Tablets and monuments of exquisite design, and some of them executed at great expense, are found all along," affirmed one 1887 tour guide. "They are to be seen standing everywhere—all over the field of strife. These, with the hundreds which will yet be erected, . . . will make the *Battle Field of Gettysburg* a place of the greatest interest upon the American continent during all ages to come."

Indeed, increasing interest in the battlefield, combined with the enormous influence that veteran's groups like the GAR now enjoyed in Washington, would lead to the federal government's assuming supervision of the area. What precipitated this takeover was a threat from one of the manifestations of progress: the electric railroad. To transport passengers more comfortably around the 25 square miles of battleground, entrepreneurs constructed such a railway, hoping to add a loop across much that was still private property embracing Confederate positions.

Fear that the railroad would forever destroy valuable historic land prompted the War Department to take increased interest in Gettysburg, urged on by constant lobbying of individuals like old General Sickles. The loss of his leg had taken none of the fight out of him. In 1891 he came to Gettysburg to speak at the dedication of the Tammany Regiment monument. Despite its growth, the battlefield had suffered from lack of funds and the necessity for continual appropriations from the several state legislatures. It needed a single, central authority to chart its course. That same year Sickles served on a committee of seven distinguished veterans who recommended federal ownership of the battlefield. In 1892 when he ran for Congress and won election, his one major issue was the battlefield. In Washington he pressed ceaselessly for national acquisition of the site.

Sickles's efforts began to bear fruit when on May 25, 1893, Congress provided $50,000 for the War Department to lay out and survey the original lines of battle—Union *and* Confederate—and to buy land for construction of roadways along the main lines. Further, tablets with historical information were to be placed throughout the battlefield, miles of additional fencing were to be added, and land deemed vital to the project was to be condemned if it could not be bought. These actions opened the way for halting further development of the electric railroad. When its backers would not voluntarily curtail their plans, a two-year battle that was finally decided in the U.S. Supreme Court settled the issue. In a landmark decision for historic preservation, the railway enterprise was stopped. The War Department acquired the necessary land, and the condemnation precedent was set for decades to come. During the next 20 years nearly 250 acres of battlefield would be acquired in similar fashion.

Gettysburg Battlefield was still not a federal preserve, but after the electric railroad controversy and the commencement of Sickles's congressional term, it was only a matter of time. Sickles helped draw up and introduce into Congress on December 18, 1894, a bill to authorize the War Department to accept ownership of some 522 acres of battlefield land with all its buildings, monuments, and improvements in addition to the remaining assets of the Gettysburg Battlefield Memorial Association. The directors of the old association recognized that their organization had done all it could. In October 1894 they voted unanimously to disband and, upon passage of the park bill, let the War Department pursue its work. On Feburary 11, 1895, the bill became law. At the same time, other Civil War battlegrounds were being similarly acquired by the War Department, an agency that could give more efficient service and coordination in developing and maintaining them.

A commission was already in place and ready to press at once for battlefield development. In 1893, as part of the War Department's plan for marking battle lines and acquiring land, a three-man commission was appointed to perform the task: Colonel John P. Nicholson, a particularly influential Pennsylvania veteran; John B. Bachelder, a historian; and General W. H. Forney. Forney was symbolic of a turning point in Gettysburg's development as well as of the War Department's attitude toward all Civil War parks. He had been a *Confederate* general. Nearly 30 years had passed since the war—time enough for wounds to heal. The government wanted to preserve the entire history of that conflict, not just one side of it. In its instructions to the commissioners the War Department explicitly directed them to identify the lines of both armies and to mark with tablets the positions of every battery, regiment, brigade, division, and corps solely "with reference to the study and correct understanding of the battle." Each tablet was to carry a brief historical synopsis of that unit's part "without praise and without censure."

The 72d Pennsylvania stood in the very midst of the holocaust of lead and iron as Pickett and his men tried to break through Meade's line on July 3. Today, near the High Water Mark, only this lone soldier swinging his clubbed musket commemorates the desperate stand of the Pennsylvanians. Here, with no protection, they stood and fired volley after volley at their attackers.

The Confederates were headed for a copse, or grove, of trees where these woods stand today. The High Water Mark Monument memorializes the farthest advance of Rebel troops and honors all those who took part in the attack and in the defense.

Already on the battlefield was a Southern monument. The state of Maryland took pride in being the first to erect a memorial. On November 19, 1886, survivors of the 2d Maryland Confederate Infantry had come to Gettysburg to unveil in a large and impressive ceremony the first and only monument commemorating the position of a Southern unit. The monument had been erected "without all thought of bitterness. Lift we then the curtain of the past." The speakers called upon their Confederate brethren to come forth now to Gettysburg "to complete the record, worthy in its entirety to be engraved 'with an iron pen, in lead, upon the rock forever.' "

One of the last events at Gettysburg during the administration of the old Battlefield Memorial Association was one of the most symbolic; in its way it heralded the War Department's new policy. On June 2, 1892, the High Water Mark of the Rebellion Monument was dedicated on the spot on Cemetery Ridge where Longstreet's assault of July 3—known as "Pickett's Charge"— had struck the Union lines. The bronze memorial, in the form of an enormous open book, lists Confederate and Union units that participated in the ill-fated attack. John Bachelder had designed the memorial. He declared, "It was here that one of the most gallant charges recorded in history terminated; here that the tide of success of the Confederacy turned. . . . This was indeed the High-Water Mark of the Rebellion."

A New Gettysburg Park

Upon transfer of jurisdiction of the battlefield, the three-man commission immediately set to work directing Gettysburg National Park, a combination of old GBMA land and new ground being acquired by the War Department. To control the patterns of that growth members of Congress passed the "Sickles Bill," which prescribed future limits of the park, identified significant pieces of land for acquisition, and stipulated that land adjacent to battle sites might also be obtained in order to preserve the appearance of the battlefield. The law set the park's limits at 3,874 acres, but changed by Act of Congress in 1990.

The former Confederate states were hopeful because of the new, impartial direction at Gettysburg. They had long harbored feelings of bitterness over restrictions on location of Southern monuments. When private parties began working to create a Chickamauga battlefield association in Georgia, outspoken Confederates and like-minded Northerners made certain that it was to be a non-partisan endeavor, citing Gettysburg as an example to avoid. Also, it was hardly surprising that many Confederates did not care to memorialize the one battle that seemed to symbolize the beginning of the decline of their cause. Nevertheless, the War Department commission earnestly encouraged the Southern states to cooperate in marking Confederate positions on the battlefield.

There arose a problem in the regulations governing location of monuments. They were to be placed only on *battle lines* occupied by regiments: For the Federal regiments at Gettysburg this was fine; acting on the defensive, they had fought on their battle lines. The Confederates, however, had had their battle lines along Seminary Ridge and north of town. They objected to placing markers there when they had actually done their fighting in front of Yankee battle lines. It proved an irresolvable dilemma. Despite repeated urgings from the Southern member of the commission, Major William Robbins, Confederate veterans refused to participate. Thus, in addition to the existing 2d Maryland marker, only one other Confederate regimental monument would ever be erected by veterans of Gettysburg. It honored the 4th Alabama, Robbins's own regiment. When his fellow veterans declined to contribute, he paid for the simple bronze tablet himself and put it up in 1904.

As for tablets to mark the positions of all other Confederate units, Robbins spent years writing the narratives for them and trying to locate accurately Confederate positions. The fruits of his work are still in evidence, as the Robbins tablets continue to provide visitors with the story of Confederate positions along their battle lines. It would be several decades, however, before the Confederate states were properly memorialized at Gettysburg in a manner comparable to the magnificent edifices that Northern states were beginning to erect.

Major Robbins had not been the only change on the commission. John Bachelder had died just before the War Department assumed administrative control. He was replaced by Major Charles Richardson, who, together with Robbins and commission chairman Nicholson, led the new Gettysburg National Park through a decade of

Dawn over Cemetery Hill is peaceful now. Yet here on July 2, 1863, a desperate Confederate assault came so close to success that Northern defenders were forced to use rocks and muskets as clubs to repulse it.

rapid expansion and extensive enhancement. Much of that progress was owing to another former Union officer, Colonel Emmor B. Cope. A career engineer, he had spent time in Gettysburg during the fall of 1863 drawing the first detailed maps of the battlefield. He had taken the post of engineer for the commissioners when they had first begun surveying the battleground in 1893 and had stayed on with the War Department administration. Eventually Cope was to become the first superintendent of the Gettysburg park, remaining for over 30 years until his death in 1927.

The commission had much work to accomplish. The several miles of "driveway" that had been constructed by the old Memorial Association lay in bad repair. Even worse, technology had made it obsolete. Visitors were now coming in ever larger numbers. Earlier visitors had been mostly veterans, who had returned to Gettysburg to relive their memories. The twentieth century brought a whole new generation of sightseers, coming to experience for themselves the place their fathers and grandfathers held so memorable. They were starting to arrive in automobiles; that alone required that the old dirt roads be resurfaced. In addition, as more land was acquired, more roads were constructed and given a more permanent surfacing. By the 1930s Gettysburg National Park contained over 30 miles of avenues bordered by some 25 miles of fencing.

Testimony to the diligence of the commissioners was the continuing addition of parcels of land. Some 800 acres came under park management in the years immediately following the War Department's take-over. Now visitors could view the Peach Orchard and walk over Houck's Ridge. They could look at the Trostle barn, the home of the Culps, and a number of other buildings that figured prominently in the famous battle.

Perhaps most impressive of all, however, were the myriad artifacts of the actual conflict. Out of storage at West Point and from government arsenals elsewhere arrived more than 300 Civil War cannon—Union and Confederate—many of them actual veterans of the battle. The commissioners had them mounted on specially manufactured cast-iron carriages, then located them about the field to mark the positions of the batteries. Once more Seminary Ridge bristled with cannon, much as it had on that hot July day when 150 Confederate guns presaged Pickett's Charge. Once more Union cannon lined Cemetery Hill and Cemetery Ridge and jutted out from their perch atop Little Round Top. Often the guns were emplaced behind stone walls that had survived the battle or beside reconstructed breastworks representing those hastily thrown together during the fight. Over five miles of these walls

The Mississippi Monument on Seminary Ridge recalls the desperate courage and sacrifices of General Lee's men.

and breastworks had been rebuilt or restored.

Part of the effort to achieve an accurate representation of the Gettysburg field as it looked in 1863 was the reforestation of much of the land. In the years since the battle many once-wooded acres had been converted into farmland, and conversely, open land had become overgrown in places. Relying upon photographs taken in 1863, and upon maps made by General Warren and memories of veterans of the battle, the commissioners embarked upon an ambitious program to plant some 17,000 trees at sites such as Ziegler's Grove. Regrowth of trees gave significance once more to place-names like McMillan Woods and Pitzer's Woods.

In order to provide the best possible overview of the rapidly expanding battleground, the commission ordered five steel observation towers built. Visitors who made the climb up their long stairs could have a bird's-eye view of the field of fighting at Culp's Hill, at Ziegler's Grove, at the northern and southern ends of Seminary Ridge, and on Big Round Top. With the century barely begun, Gettysburg already exemplified the best-marked and most fully interpreted battlefield in the world.

Giant markers and monuments continued to arrive from their respective states. Other types of monuments were also starting to appear. By 1913 there were five magnificent bronze equestrian statues honoring General Meade and all of his corps commanders except Oliver O. Howard, George Sykes, and, ironically, Daniel Sickles. Where Generals Reynolds and Warren once stood alone on the field, they were now joined by similar statues of several other officers such as General John Buford, who had first met the Confederates in the opening hours of the struggle. Among these military men were likenesses of noncombatants as well. There was Father William Corby, whose statue took its place in 1910 on Cemetery Ridge, near the spot where he had reportedly exhorted men of the famed Irish Brigade before they had gone into battle. He had declared that the Catholic Church would refuse absolution to any man who ran from the enemy. Seven years earlier another civilian had come to stand in bronze on McPherson Ridge. He was old John Burns, a septuagenarian citizen of Gettysburg who had taken up his musket and marched out from his home to fight for the Union.

The Gettysburg National Park Commission began to erect special memorials of its own. The first was the Army of the Potomac Memorial, dedicated in 1908, on Cemetery Ridge close to

Standing at the place where he helped save the battle for the Union, General Gouverneur K. Warren gazes from Little Round Top.

the High Water Mark. The commissioners' most visible additions were their historical tablets and markers. Ironically, these markers—pedestals of granite with bronze plaques attached—went up first for the Confederates.

The commissioners then embarked upon the same task for the Federals. Even here they did not stop, for the members of the commission were determined to identify sites of Union corps field hospitals and headquarters for both armies. The laborious work of researching and preparing the hundreds of iron narrative tablets continued unabated. The narratives were part of a dream of the long-dead Colonel Bachelder. He had envisioned that through these tablets the entire battlefield would one day become "an easily read object lesson," a place not just for touring, but also for learning.

OVERLEAF: From the shade of the Copse of Trees, Cemetery Ridge runs gently toward the Round Tops. Here Lee's army was shattered, never to recover.

Fiftieth Reunion

By 1913 and the advent of the fiftieth anniversary of the battle, Gettysburg was more than ready for what would prove to be, outside of the actual encounter, the most remarkable gathering of men ever to assemble in the little Pennsylvania town. It had all started with H. S. Huidekoper of Philadelphia, a member of the Grand Army of the Republic and a veteran of the battle. In April 1908 he had suggested to Governor Edwin Stuart that the fiftieth anniversary be marked by a mammoth reunion of the men in both blue and gray at the battlefield itself. The governor received the idea warmly, established a commission to plan the affair, and appropriated $400,000 to help with expenses. Soon thereafter the federal government appropriated an additional $195,000 and offered the use of 1,500 officers and men from the army to operate the encampment that would house the veterans.

The reunion took five years of planning and the cooperation of veterans' groups and state legislatures from all over the nation, north and south. A host of veterans of Gettysburg took leading parts in planning the week-long encampment. Among them was General Joshua L. Chamberlain, who, with his 20th Maine, had helped hold Little Round Top on July 2, 1863. And heading the list, as always, was the irrepressible Dan Sickles. He regarded Gettysburg as almost his own private preserve.

Back in 1893 Sickles had met with other prominent veterans of the battle, both Union and Confederate. His fellow corps commander General O. O. Howard was in attendance. Present was General David McM. Gregg, who had stopped Confederate cavalry east of the battlefield. Also on hand were Confederates such as scrappy little General "Billy" Mahone of Virginia

PENNSYLVANIA HISTORICAL AND MUSEUM COMMISSION PHOTO

Hands clasped now in friendship, old adversaries met on the battlefield at the fiftieth reunion. One-legged General Daniel Sickles had become as venerable an institution as the battlefield itself. He had fought for years to build and strengthen the park. It is his memorial as well as that of all other veterans of Gettysburg.

Every man who fought at Gettysburg inscribed his name on the roll of bravery. Years after the battle Pennsylvania went a step further by erecting the Pennsylvania Memorial, its base lined with bronze plaques listing the name of every native son who had fought the battle in volunteer state regiments.

and General E. P. Alexander, Longstreet's artillery chief in the battle. General James Longstreet, who had led the assault forces that had destroyed Sickles's corps and then had shattered themselves in the next day's charge, was there too. Longstreet and Sickles became friends. Now, all of these former soldiers wanted that same warming experience of comradeship for the thousands of veterans still alive.

On June 29, 1913, the old warriors began to arrive. Their numbers were astounding. By the end of the week over 55,000 former Yankees and Rebels swelled the enormous tent city that had been built. Not surprisingly, Pennsylvanians made up the bulk of them: 22,103 to be exact, 303 of whom were Confederate veterans. Yet men came from all but 2 of the 48 states. To house them they found a small metropolis of 5,000 tents staked out in Union and Confederate camps on the battlefield. Nearby stood a gigantic "Great Tent" that could seat nearly 14,000. Here most of the formal indoor ceremonies were to take place. There were field hospitals staffed with doctors and nurses on call at all hours. Telephones had been installed throughout the encampment so that the old men could keep in contact with their families back home. That week most of them ate better than they ever had as soldiers. They consumed over 200 tons of meat, poultry, and vegetables; 25,000 dozen eggs; 7,000 pies; 6 tons of coffee; and some 2,000 gallons of ice cream!

An aged Yankee playfully cuffs a smiling Johnny Reb at the 1913 reunion. Fifty years before, there had been weapons in their fists.

The work of readying the battlefield for the reunion was a task on a par with waging a campaign. Quartermaster's and commissary headquarters rose beside the tent city for the veterans.

PENNSYLVANIA HISTORICAL AND MUSEUM COMMISSION PHOTO

When the old warriors
gathered, they acted like
soldiers of all times and all
nations, gathering to talk of
the old times and to refight
without malice their old battles.
With dimmed, forgiving
memories of old age, they
recalled the greatest moment
of their generation.

During Civil War days
these old soldiers would
have regarded this meal
as a feast beyond descrip-
tion. The whole reunion
was for them a feast of old
times and old comrades—
and new friends found
among old enemies.
Though they were sup-
posed to mess and camp
by states, the men of
North and South mingled
continually.

29

A small army of Boy Scouts were on hand to act as escorts and companions for the more aged or infirm, while Pennsylvania statepolicemen and contingents of the U.S. Army provided security. Army field ovens were used to cook the meals, and the veterans were all issued blankets, mess kits, lanterns, and cots. Further, for most of them transportation to the reunion had been provided free of charge. Pennsylvania railroads alone carried over 20,000 passengers gratis to and from the reunion.

Some of the old soldiers were as young as 62. Young John Clem, only 11 years old in 1862, had won national renown as the "Drummer Boy of Shiloh." Now, here he was at Gettysburg. So was old Micyah Weiss, at 112 the oldest man present. Miraculously, with all these veterans gathered in the blistering hot sun of July, there were only nine deaths, all of them Union veterans.

The old veterans turned tourist on the battleground that had become a park. A Pennsylvanian could point with pride to his name on a tablet on the Pennsylvania Monument, while men of Blue and Grey alike could take pride in the immortal words of the Gettysburg Address on the Lincoln Address Memorial.

Canes and walking sticks had taken the places of rifles and bayonets as the "boys" still remembered how they brandished their weapons.

Mostly, the veterans toured the field of battle itself. From the summit of Little Round Top they could point to Devil's Den and beyond, and back through time.

It was a glorious time for them. Camped together by states, they refused to remain still. Those who could walk ambled through all the camps, Union *and* Confederate. Those who could not, used the 400 wheelchairs made available for the event or held on tightly to the arms of a couple of sturdy Boy Scouts. The Blue and the Gray mingled with feelings of warmth and respect that none present would ever forget. Dignitaries from all across the nation came to witness this wonderful event, and President Woodrow Wilson himself made the Fourth of July address.

Nonetheless, the veterans were more interested in what their battlefield had to tell. They wandered all over it. Every day hundreds of men in blue squinted with failing eyes at the plaques on the base of the Pennsylvania Monument, each hunting for his own name in bronze. In the cemetery they visited the new Lincoln Memorial to read the words of the Gettysburg Address. To the south they climbed out onto the rocks on the crest of Little Round Top. The encampment rang with martial music, perhaps a little off key now, as old musicians got out their drums and fifes to play Civil War marching tunes. Bandsmen of the

A few could still wield other tools of their youth, like fife and drum, to serenade their camp mates and recall a time when the feet of thousands marched to their tunes.

Not all the veterans at the reunion were men. A host of nurses had participated during and after the battle, and a few were here again. Clarissa Dye sits at left, and next to her are Cornelia Hanwik, Salome Stewart, and Mary Stevens. Theirs, too, had been a role of honor. Not a few of the veterans at the reunion owed their lives to nurses like these.

Perhaps the most poignant moment of the fiftieth reunion came when these aged veterans of Pickett's Charge walked and ran a few hundred feet toward Cemetery Ridge. On this same ground as young men they had faced the full fury of Meade's defense in the most well known infantry assault of the war.

There was a new generation to learn of the deeds of the old. On July 2, 1913, one elderly veteran tells his grandson how it was half a century before.

Blue and the Gray joined together to march along the park's avenues as in days of old. Thousands stood beside the markers and monuments that gave testimony to what they had achieved here, posing for local photographers and for other veterans armed with cameras.

Even old veterans who had not actually taken part in the Gettysburg battle joined in the spirit of the occasion. General Bennett Young, a Kentucky Confederate who had not participated in the conflict, but who now commanded the United Confederate Veterans, spoke for all Confederates. "I am more than half a thousand miles from my home," he observed, "but all the same I am home. In this land everywhere is my home." Then he led the assembled Confederates in a stirring salute to their new friends and their Pennsylvania hosts by giving them "something that no one else in the world can give you . . . the Rebel Yell." The Great Tent shook with the thunderous sound.

The high point of the reunion, the moment that strained every heart to its utmost, came on July 3 when 150 old Confederates reenacted the great assault on Cemetery Ridge. It was too far for them to walk all the way from their original lines on Seminary Ridge, so they began a hundred yards or so in front of the stone wall near the High Water Mark. Awaiting them behind that wall were the 180 remaining members of Federal units that had met the attack in 1863. General Sickles, tears welling in his eyes, sat nearby, watching intently as the Southerners reached the

All around the veterans on the field were other old friends, now only motionless shadows in bronze. Men of valor like Major General John Sedgwick rose in beautiful equestrian monuments to stir the memories of their former comrades. Sedgwick sits astride his horse on the site of his headquarters.

wall. No fighting now, but a shaking of hands, exchanges of greetings, weeping, and the solemn and symbolic offering to the Confederates of the Stars and Stripes.

Later that evening both sides cheered and applauded enthusiastically at an immense fireworks display on Little Round Top. After the final spectacle, symbolic of the new century was the procession of over 14,000 automobiles, headlamps piercing the night, as spectators drove back to Gettysburg. The next day the reunion ended with President Wilson's speech, the tolling of bells in Gettysburg, and a final sounding of taps before thousands of old men proudly standing at attention. Then it was time to return home; the reunion had been an incredible success. The greatest star of all had been Gettysburg National Military Park. Not even the coming Revolutionary sesquicentennial celebration in 1931 at Yorktown would be such an affair, and never before had a government preserve been so ready.

The encampment had meant so much to the old soldiers because a major portion of the battleground looked to them exactly as it had 50 years before. None of them could be immune to the thrill of seeing the deeds of their youth commemorated on a field filled with magnificent monuments, many of them examples of the finest sculpture of the time. For instance, the artistry of Henry Kirke Bush-Brown in his inspiring equestrian statues of Meade, Reynolds, and Sedgwick, was regarded by art critics as among the finest in the nation. The General Slocum statue was designed by Edward Clark Potter, a prominent sculptor in the 1890s. The imposing New York Artillery monument was executed by Caspar Buberl, who sculpted the simple but eloquent New York Battery monument as well. Everywhere the old veterans could see their deeds of blood and pain remembered now in quiet and dignity. The battlefield did more than merely keep alive their memories; it softened them and fostered the most pleasant. It offered the veterans and their posterity an imposing memorial of beauty and majesty.

The 1913 reunion also brought still another

art form to Gettysburg, though not at first to the park. In 1882 French artist Paul Philippoteaux came to Gettysburg to talk with veterans of the battle and make sketches of the terrain. What he had in mind was an enormous circular painting depicting the climactic moments on July 3 when the Confederate assault was threatening to penetrate the Union line. Returning to Paris, he spent the next three years working with five assistants to create one of the most remarkable representations ever painted. It stood 50 feet high and 400 feet in circumference. The Gettysburg "Cyclorama" was meticulous in its detail, generally accurate, and vivid in its portrayal of the heroism and tragedy of that bloody day. Philippoteaux sent his masterpiece to Boston, but in 1913 it was brought to Gettysburg where it really belonged—its transfer spurred in part, no doubt, by the increasing number of visitors to the park. Here for the next 49 years it hung in a damp, unheated exhibit building where the elements and neglect threatened to destroy it.

At last it was time to go. "Good-bye, comrade. God be with you!" a battle-scarred Yank wished his Southern friend. They were the end of an era.

The departing veterans left behind a military park that symbolized all they had fought for, all they remembered, and all they hoped to bequeath to posterity. Behind them they also left enduring images of their struggle and old heroes like General Meade, mounted on "Old Baldy," to guard their hallowed ground.

Echoes of Another War: Camp Colt

There was much in danger of destruction after 1913. Europe had become embroiled in the Great War, and it was only a few years before America, too, sounded the call to arms. With the coming again of war, Gettysburg once more echoed to the tread of marching feet. In fact, harking back to its early days in managing the park, the War Department envisioned Gettysburg and other Civil War battlefields as more than historic sites. It viewed them as places for military lessons and training as well. The military war colleges studied Civil War campaigns intently; and every May the senior class from the U.S. Military Academy at West Point spent several days on the Gettysburg battleground studying its strategic and tactical features before writing theses on the subject.

With America's entry into World War I, the War Department established Camp Colt in the fields over which Longstreet's Confederates had charged on July 3, 1863. The 4th, 7th, 58th, 59th, 60th, and 61st U.S. Infantry units were sent there from Texas to begin training before going overseas. In May of 1917 the battlefield began to reverberate with sounds of recruits being turned into soldiers, and in 1918 tank service units began to train and practice maneuvers within the park. The young trainees must have felt a certain eeriness about preparing for conflict in a place so haunted by memories of another war. It was not just their own officers who watched them at their schooling; in addition, they marched under the vigilant eyes of Meade and Hancock and Warren.

And now, at last, other eyes observed too— Confederate eyes. For on June 8, 1917, Virginia had become the first Southern state to erect a major memorial honoring all her sons in that crucial battle. It had taken ten years from the time that Virginia's Confederate veterans had petitioned their legislature to appropriate funds to erect a suitable memorial at Gettysburg. A compe-tition had been announced and sculptors the world over were solicited to submit two designs: one including General Robert E. Lee and one without him. This requirement seemed strange as Lee was so indelibly etched in the Virginian mind that no memorial could be conceived of as complete without him.

The winning design was entered by William Sievers, who combined both concepts into one by suggesting a giant pedestal surmounted by an equestrian statue of Lee, and at its base a grouping in bronze representing in a heroic pose the various arms of the Confederate military. Thus he would memorialize both Lee and the common soldiers of Virginia. The sculpture cost some $50,000. When the day arrived for the unveiling, it was Lee's granddaughter who drew away the covering. Now Southern boys drilling for war out on those fields could look toward Seminary Ridge, to the spot where Lee had commanded his greatest attack, and behold his likeness sitting in quiet dignity astride his horse Traveler.

The Virginia Memorial finally broke the reluctance of the Southern states to erect memorials at Gettysburg. With World War I ended, several other states began their work. There were not enough veterans left now to attempt the sort of regimental memorials placed by Union outfits. Rather, the South sought state by state to publicly fund and dedicate single monuments to all their sons. In so doing, they quietly vied with their former foes in commissioning the most beautiful and impressive works of art. Still, it was another 12 years before the next memorial, the North Carolina Monument, came to the field. The creation of Gutzon Borglum, it proved radically different from all other state edifices in the park.

Already one of the leading sculptors in the country, Borglum was just commencing work on his colossal creation, the Mount Rushmore

Happily, there was much more in store for the military park. Although fewer and fewer veterans would return in coming years, more of them would appear in bronze, like these Tarheels in Gutzon Borglum's magnificent North Carolina Monument, about to charge once more toward Cemetery Ridge and immortality.

presidential monument, when he accepted North Carolina's commission. His intention, he stated, was to depict a group of Tarheel soldiers as if they had "just been ordered forward to charge across that very bloody battlefield." He made a bronze grouping of five figures, enlisted soldiers poised in a forward position, advancing with their colors into the charge. North Carolina placed the monument on Seminary Ridge only a few hundred yards north of the Virginia Monument, at the place where North Carolinians had formed their battle lines. This memorial was dedicated on July 3, 1929.

The year 1933 was a watershed year for all of the Civil War parks scattered around the country. In that year the War Department transferred them to the jurisdiction of the National Park Service, and they became *national* military parks. For

nearly 40 years the War Department had developed and managed Gettysburg with sensitivity and dedication to fairness and accuracy. Prior to 1933 a visitor center of sorts had been created on an upper floor of the Gettysburg post office. In it were displayed artifacts and giant relief maps, designed and constructed under the supervision of Engineer Emmor Cope, which illustrated the battleground.

Under federal guidance the old park had expanded markedly. There were now 2,116 acres of park land to be conveyed to the National Park Service, along with the National Cemetery. Nearly 900 monuments and some 415 cannon were in place. For the past 17 years the War Department had authorized special civilian guides to conduct tourists through the battleground. No one could become a guide without first being

Dozens of Civil War–period buildings still dot the Gettysburg landscape. Farmhouses like the George Weikert home evoke images of the simple country town made immortal by the passing of the armies.

tested and licensed by the superintendent—a practice that has continued to the present. Of all the Civil War parks Gettysburg was the showplace, and such it would remain. But there would be hard years ahead for the park and for the nation.

With the country in the throes of the Great Depression, facilities like national parks would at first seem to be a low priority. However, Gettysburg and other parks actually benefited from federal programs created to employ many thousands of people out of work during that era. New Deal agencies like the Civilian Conservation Corps provided work for several thousand. Scores of them lived at Gettysburg through the 1930s, staying in camps in the Pitzer and McMillan woods and working under the supervision of the National Park Service and CCC managers. They carried on snow removal in winter and at other seasons performed landscaping and foliage maintenance, road building, cleaning of monuments, and repair of aging battlefield buildings. Thanks to CCC aid, the park emerged from the Depression in better condition than before, with new drainage facilities, polished and more readable markers, buildings sporting new paint, and roads free of potholes.

SEVENTY-FIFTH REUNION

The refurbishing could not have been better timed. Twenty-five years had slipped past since the 1913 reunion, and a movement was well under way to provide for a seventy-fifth encampment. Indeed, the impetus for it had originated at the fiftieth anniversary reunion, when attending veterans agreed that they should meet again

to dedicate a lasting memorial to peace among themselves.

Like the earlier reunion, the 1938 meeting required a great deal of planning and preparation. Pennsylvania chartered a commission to lay plans for the event, aided by a federal commission. Paul Roy, editor of *The Gettysburg Times*, accepted the post of executive secretary. It was he who journeyed to Texas in 1935 to address the convention of the United Confederate Veterans and to invite their participation. At first they were not enthusiastic, owing to opposition from their longtime leader Harry R. Lee. But within a few days the editor managed to change Lee's mind and win enthusiastic approval by Southern veterans. Diplomacy also persuaded the reluctant Grand Army of the Republic to endorse the reunion.

The veterans had grown quite old; some of them were over a hundred. There was little enthusiasm for the arduous trip to Gettysburg, and in the depths of the Depression few could afford the economic expenditure that attendance at such a convention would require. But support for the reunion gradually increased, and by June 29, 1938, the opening day, it was already destined to be a grand success.

There were far fewer of the old soldiers now. Whereas the 55,000 Civil War veterans who had attended the 1913 affair were by no means all of those then living, by 1938 there were fewer than 12,000 in the entire country. Of these, 3,600 accepted invitations to attend the encampment; about 2,000 actually made the journey to Gettysburg. When the elders arrived they found another tent city, not so large this time, located on land near Gettysburg College. Everything necessary

The veterans did come once more, in 1938 for the seventy-fifth anniversary. There were fewer of them now, but not so few that they could not still clasp hands in friendship across the stone wall at the Angle. There, the bitter hand-to-hand fighting at the climax of Pickett's Charge virtually ended the bloodiest battle ever fought on the American continent.

for the comfort and care of the old-timers—almost all of them over ninety—was provided. Every veteran was assigned a special attendant to see to his needs and be ready at all times if assistance in walking should be needed. Attendants, like the veterans, were provided free transportation to the battlefield and received modest pay for their services. In addition, the Commonwealth of Pennsylvania placed National Guard troopers at the camp to join with the Boy Scouts, Red Cross, and other charitable organizations to help conduct the encampment.

There was something different about the spirit at this reunion. The veterans were all nearing the end of their life. Their country and the world were close to global war, the likes of which fighting men of 1863 could never have imagined. Indeed, during the reunion there were tangible examples of the growing effort of America to arm herself. The Army had set up an exhibition area to display and demonstrate its latest weapons, including antiaircraft guns that dramatized the fact that war could now rain from the skies. Soldiers of the 12th Infantry and other units paraded in town. On the Fourth of July there was a major military parade that included not only infantry but also battalions of tanks. A regimental cavalry

charge demonstrated the Army's long-lasting tradition of fielding units ill-equipped for modern warfare.

Amid all this militant pageantry it was more than fitting that the theme throughout the reunion was peace. The high point of the encampment came on the evening of July 3 when the Eternal Light Peace Memorial was dedicated on Oak Hill. Back at the 1913 encampment the idea for such a memorial had been conceived. Pennsylvania had called for laying the cornerstone of such a monument as part of the ceremonies and had proposed to the United Confederate Veterans that they combine forces in a joint effort. More plans were formulated in the Great Tent during the fiftieth reunion, and there the Gettysburg Peace Memorial Association was formed. The association's aim was to obtain from Congress the appointment of a special commission with a suitable appropriation to erect on the battlefield a "peace monument" commemorating the fiftieth reunion and the spirit of brotherhood in the nation. The appropriation did not come in time for a cornerstone to be set in 1913, but by 1938 the funds had been provided. The Eternal Light Peace Memorial was constructed.

President Franklin D. Roosevelt came to

Gettysburg, along with an estimated 200,000 spectators, to unveil the memorial, which had been draped with an enormous flag. After a brief address the President gave a signal that sent the Stars and Stripes plummeting into the outstretched arms of a Union veteran and a Confederate veteran, aided by Pennsylvania National Guardsmen. Etched into the stone facing of the memorial were the words "PEACE ETERNAL IN A NATION UNITED." Then, atop the memorial a flame was lit to burn eternally, a symbol of America's peace with itself and its hope for peace with all nations. The next day's military maneuvers, despite their air of pomp and festivity, impressed upon many in attendance that they might soon have to fight for the right to keep that flame burning.

POSTWAR DEVELOPMENTS

The advent of World War II naturally diverted national attention from Gettysburg, though some progress was still made. In 1941 the Park Service acquired the Cyclorama. Sometime prior to that year the first governmentally authorized guides to Gettysburg National Military Park had been written and printed. Before then, visitors had had to rely upon privately published, often highly inaccurate guidebooks, the first of which had been published in the 1880s. During the Second World War, park staff began for the first time to set up field exhibits that supplemented the memorial markers and tablets. A program of planned historical interpretation of the battlefield began to evolve.

Meanwhile, manifestations of the war in Europe were also evident in the United States. For the large numbers of German and Italian prisoners of war the War Department established several prison camps in Pennsylvania—one on ground now a part of the Gettysburg park. It must have been a sobering experience for some of those prisoners, finding themselves watched not only by their guards, but also by the unblinking eyes of bronze statues of generals like Lee and Meade. This sensation would have been felt all the more keenly by soldiers in the German Army who, before this war, may have studied Civil War tactics, particularly those at Gettysburg.

Return to peacetime found some major changes imminent for Gettysburg Battlefield. Visitation increased as America entered the 1950s. Other postwar influences promised not only to give the park more usage, but also to threaten its integrity. Booming suburban development, like that occurring all across the country, began to edge ever closer to the battlefield. Homes were started on Oak Ridge. At Colt Park a development actually began to threaten part of the Pickett's Charge field. Housing tracts appeared along the Emmitsburg Road, endangering sites like the Wheatfield and the Peach Orchard.

That was not all. The park's very attraction to Americans was posing for it a multitude of new problems and dangers. In the mid-1960s the

influx of new residents was minuscule compared to the flow of tourists—visitors who needed food and lodging. Better highways had made it easier for travelers to get to Gettysburg. In no time the annual visitation count soared above one million. Within only a few years some streets, particularly Steinwehr Avenue, which runs through the Pickett's Charge area, sprouted a variety of motels, restaurants, and private museums. Commercial development, dependent upon the battlefield for its lifeblood, was actually threatening destruction of much of the scenic impact.

Meanwhile, as additional pieces of land were acquired, the battleground continued to expand. More monuments and markers went up, though fewer now. In 1956 a bronze statue was erected in Ziegler's Grove to honor Albert Woolson, the last Union veteran of the Civil War to die. His passing signaled the end of an era; it came, appropriately enough, at the beginning of another. For the United States was even then gearing up for yet another celebration that would involve Gettysburg National Military Park in a leading role: the Civil War Centennial.

CENTENNIAL

In the 1950s the National Park Service had begun a service-wide program, entitled "Mission 66," to repair and improve park lands and buildings that of necessity had been neglected while the country's resources were channeled toward the war effort. In addition to refurbishing them, Mission 66 prepared the parks—Gettysburg among them—for a dramatic increase in visitation. With the Centennial approaching, Civil War parks received special attention and were managed with an extra sense of urgency. At Gettysburg a large-scale program was initiated of resurfacing avenues for vehicular traffic. More field exhibits were planned. Park staff laid out a new High Water Mark walking tour, put up a bridge over the Railroad Cut near McPherson's Ridge, and wrote an entirely new battlefield guidebook.

Even more ambitious was the plan for a new visitor center. The old museum in the downtown post office had been obsolete for years. The

Like so many battlefield parks, Gettysburg began largely with the National Cemetery, itself in part an outgrowth of Evergreen Cemetery, where more than one Federal had taken shelter behind a headstone.

To help honor them all, the new Cyclorama Center was built in 1962, barely a few score yards from the battle line of July 3.

park needed a building designed specifically for its own special uses. Architect Richard Neutra received the commission to create a new visitor center that would also house the now aging and delicate Cyclorama. He conceived a building which, though controversial when opened in 1962, was still attractive and functional. It combined in one structure on Cemetery Ridge a museum, a theater, a scenic overlook balcony, National Park Service offices, and a giant "drum" to house the Cyclorama. Nestled in trees just behind the battle line, the new visitor center served as the starting point for the driving tour of the battlefield. Not only did it offer a film and a narrative depicting the drama of Philippoteaux's painting, it also provided a series of excellent exhibits.

Other War Department programs were expanded to return the battlefield to its rural atmosphere of 1863. For example, farmers now rent a large portion of the land, planting crops that may have been growing there at the time of the conflict. This agricultural permit program considerably reduced park maintenance and at the same time aided interpretation.

As the Centennial neared, private sources provided assistance with land acquisitions intended to halt commercialism creeping toward the battlefield. In August 1959 Gettysburg College held a conference on the Civil War. Some of the "buffs" and historians in attendance proposed that they do something to halt advancing encroachment. They identified over 1,000 acres of historically significant battlefield land occupied by motels or refreshment stands or in danger of being put to such use. Out of their discussions grew the Gettysburg Battlefield Preservation Association.

In the four years prior to the Centennial, the association managed to raise funds and purchase for donation well over a hundred acres, including ground over which Confederates had advanced to attack Little Round Top and a 118-acre tract that was the scene of much of the first day's fighting. All told, they acquired 180 acres by 1963, and since then they have continued to donate parcels of land. Similarly, private groups like the Military Order of the Loyal Legion (a patriotic and historical organization created by Union veterans in 1865 and continued by descendants and other interested persons) have given land. The W. Alton Jones Foundation donated 264 acres.

When the Centennial opened in 1961, Gettysburg National Military Park, with over 2,800 acres, was approaching the 3,874-acre limitation imposed by the old Sickles plan. Sadly, large and important tracts of land such as the East Cavalry Field, three miles east of town, could not be acquired because they would expand the park over its limit.

The Centennial spurred more states, all of them Confederate, to erect monuments. Meanwhile, on the field itself park personnel were enhancing the interpretation of existing properties and correcting a few long-standing errors. In July of 1963, as a fitting end of the observance, the park hosted a reenactment of the battle. Gettysburg National Military Park emerged from the fanfare and commercialism of this four-year Civil War Centennial with its Mission 66 work nearly complete and its programs for the public improved. Ahead lay more challenges and new opportunities.

LATER EXPANSION AND IMPROVEMENTS

As the park entered the late 1960s and the 1970s, the earlier days of Superintendents Nicholson, Bachelder, and Cope might have seemed like a happy dream. Surrounding business enterprises were growing ever closer to the battlefield as more and more entrepreneurs sought to provide services and entertainment for the millions who journeyed here. With federal emphasis now shifting away from Civil War parks toward preparation for the Revolutionary War Bicentennial, funds for additional acquisitions became limited.

Nonetheless, the 1970s saw still more monuments unveiled.

There arose a threat so menacing to the park environment that it commanded national headlines for months. In 1970 a proposal was made that a 330-foot observation tower be built by business interests on privately owned Cemetery Hill property. The National Park Service protested at once, calling the tower a "monstrosity." Partly as a reaction to this response, the tower developers abandoned their first site and instead suggested erecting the structure just outside of the park's boundary. The crux of the matter was that a 300-foot tower would dominate Gettysburg's otherwise rural skyline—a visual intrusion from almost every vantage point in the park. Its impact on the park's environment and ambience would be enormous.

A year later, in a move that surprised most observers, the Department of the Interior attempted to make the best of a bad situation. The department negotiated an agreement that allowed the developers right-of-way through park land if they would build their tower at a distance behind Cemetery Hill. A few days later the Commonwealth of Pennsylvania initiated legal action to stop the tower's construction altogether. After more than two years of litigation, the state lost the case. In the summer of 1974 the tower was completed and opened for business.

Despite its adverse impact on the scenic beauty of the battleground, park officials called the tower "the single, most important factor in stimulating a renewed interest in Gettysburg, the catalytic agent that stirred the collective conscience and drew attention to an area never forgotten but recently ignored." As a result, the Advisory Council on Historic Preservation set to work to study special problems faced by Gettysburg. A variety of pressures on the battlefield were to be examined: increased highway traffic, needs of businessmen in the community, the impact of local township and county agencies, and the effect of the newly formed Historic Gettysburg–Adams County, Incorporated. The Advisory Council was to find some means of coordinating the services and needs of all these factors.

Even before the tower controversy had found its resolution, the park was coping with another commercial intrusion. One of the earliest private museums in Gettysburg was the Rosensteel family's Gettysburg National Museum. It had grown out of a private collection of battleground artifacts collected shortly after the fighting ended and had expanded rapidly over the years. In 1921

The ground around Bloody Run (or Plum Run) at the foot of Little Round Top was acquired by the War Department, incorporated into the park, and recently returned to its 1863 appearance by the National Park Service. A granite soldier from the 40th New York Infantry silently guards this place in history.

the family had opened their museum directly across the street from the west entrance to the National Cemetery. They added to their collection an "electric map" presentation that showed the movements of the armies at Gettysburg.

By 1970 the National Museum housed one of the largest collections of Civil War weapons and artifacts in the nation. In 1972 the National Park Service bought the museum and its collection and began converting it from a private enterprise into a public service. Eastern National Park and Monument Association, a nonprofit organization working with the National Park Service, took over management of the building and the electric map, installed a Civil War bookstore, and helped pave the way for the museum's conversion into the new principal visitor center.

SUGGESTED READING

CATTON, BRUCE. *Gettysburg: The Final Fury.* Garden City, New York: Doubleday and Co., 1974.

Civil War Times Illustrated. *Gettysburg.* With articles by Edward J. Stackpole *et al.* Reprint. Philadelphia: Eastern Acorn Press, 1981.

CODDINGTON, EDWIN B. *Gettysburg Campaign: A Study in Command.* Reprint. Dayton, Ohio: Press of Morningside Bookshop, 1979.

COHEN, STAN. *Hands Across the Wall: The 50th and 75th Reunions of the Gettysburg Battle.* Charleston, West Virginia: Pictorial Histories Publishing Company, 1982.

FRASSANITO, WILLIAM A. *Gettysburg: A Journey in Time.* New York: Charles Scribner's Sons, 1975.

TILBERG, FREDERICK. *Gettysburg National Military Park, Pennsylvania.* U.S. National Park Service Historical Handbook Series, No. 9. Rev. ed. Washington, D.C.: U.S. Government Printing Office, 1962.

TUCKER, GLENN. *High Tide at Gettysburg: The Campaign in Pennsylvania.* Rev. ed. Dayton, Ohio: Press of Morningside Bookshop, 1973.

Gettysburg National Military Park Today

More than a century after the battle, Gettysburg is a high-water mark in the nation's effort to preserve the scenes of its undying past.

Gettysburg has a story to offer that covers more than the Civil War; it spans two centuries and two great conflicts. Adjacent to the park now is the Eisenhower National Historic Site. During the First World War Dwight D. Eisenhower, then a captain, commanded Camp Colt here, training recruits for overseas. He found that he liked Gettysburg, but it was not until more than 30 years later, after he had retired from the Army in 1950, that he took up residence. In 1951 the Eisenhowers bought a 189-acre farm that adjoined park land just west of Seminary Ridge. There in 1953 they began remodeling the existing house, and later in 1955 they moved in and started raising livestock on the farm.

During the two terms that he served as president, Eisenhower continued to use the Gettysburg farm as a retreat. When he left office in 1961, it was here that he and Mamie came to spend their remaining years. In 1967, shortly before the former president's death, the Eisenhowers donated the farm to the U.S. government. After Mrs. Eisenhower died in November 1979, the Park Service assumed management of the home and its contents. A shuttle-bus service was inaugurated to take visitors to the farm. Park interpreters are now available to assist visitors in touring the house, which still contains many of the Eisenhowers' furnishings and mementos including several of the President's paintings.

Even as the park has continued to expand its holdings, it has also recognized the necessity of improving and safeguarding what it already owns. The tower controversy of the early 1970s made it abundantly clear that the park's surroundings were almost as important in maintaining the desired ambience for Gettysburg as the park lands themselves. In 1975 the Gettysburg Battlefield Historic District, comprising over 20,000 acres of land was designated; it was then entered into the National Register of Historic Places. This status at least preserves these lands from intrusion by federally funded projects.

In June 1977 the Advisory Council on Historic Preservation, which had begun studying the special problems faced by Gettysburg, submitted a plan for preserving historic resources of the Gettysburg area, both within and outside the park boundaries. It recognized that:

> The problem with Gettysburg National Military Park, Gettysburg National Cemetery, and Eisenhower National Historic Site is that while, with certain exceptions, much of the land that is historic . . . is contained within park boundaries, most of the setting for this land is not.

The means to preserve these national sites, it concluded, lay not so much with the National Park Service as with the civic jurisdictions that surrounded them: the Borough of Gettysburg; Cumberland and Staban Townships; and Adams County, Pennsylvania. Unless these agencies and the park could in some fashion work together with an eye to their mutual benefit, Gettysburg stood to suffer even more glaring incursions into its historical setting. To meet these and other challenges, park officials continue their task of

So long as Robert E. Lee gazes across the fields where his army marched to glory, Americans will remember Gettysburg.

Here, too, a great man of another era is remembered. Eisenhower National Historic Site is ample testimony to the lure that Gettysburg held for a distinguished general. Eisenhower left the field of battle and the halls of the White House for the lush countryside of his farmhouse at the southern end of Seminary Ridge.

finding the best methods of preserving their holdings and of adding to them.

Gettysburg National Military Park has moved on into the 1990s. Boundary legislation in 1990 increased the park to 5,883 acres, and it encompasses more than 100 buildings, 8.5 miles of rock walls and historic defenses, over 30 miles of roadways, and more than 1,320 monuments and informational tablets. Though it is not the largest of our Civil War parks, Gettysburg is without question the one most visited.

Every year over one million persons come to tour Gettysburg Battlefield and to take advantage of the variety of programs offered. In the amphitheater located just west of Seminary Ridge visitors attend evening ranger programs. They travel the hiking and biking trails that extend throughout the park. They may make the historic walk across the fields between Seminary and Cemetery ridges and retrace the steps of Longstreet's assault. To view the battlefield they may climb the remaining old War Department observation towers on Culp's Hill, Oak Hill, and Seminary Ridge. They may direct their course to the Eternal Light Peace Memorial and examine a Whitworth breechloader—an English-made Confederate cannon—placed nearby. In the National

Touring Gettysburg National Military Park

An absorbing historical experience awaits those who want to tour the battlefield at their own pace.

1. High Water Mark
2. Pennsylvania Memorial
3. Little Round Top
4. Devil's Den
5. The Wheatfield
6. The Peach Orchard
7. Pitzer Woods
8. Virginia Memorial
9. North Carolina Memorial
10. McPherson Ridge
11. Eternal Light Peace Memorial
12. Oak Ridge
13. Barlow Knoll
14. Culp's Hill View
15. Spangler's Spring
16. Cemetery Hill
17. National Cemetery

Cemetery they may stroll along the quiet rows of graves, reading from cast-iron tablets as they go the verses of Theodore O'Hara's immortal poem "The Bivouac of the Dead."

It has been 130 years since David McConaughy took the first tentative steps toward memorializing what had occurred at Gettysburg in July 1863. In the intervening decades Gettysburg has faced and survived challenges, changes, and threats. Through it all the park and the town have progressed, conscious of the special place they occupy in the minds and hearts of Americans north and south. Gettysburg is far from the forgotten little farm community it was in 1863; it can never return entirely to that stage. But for those who come here there is something of a journey back in time, to a site where armies converged and where men gallantly rose above themselves.

A century ago, in 1886, a visitor came to Gettysburg and gazed across the fields where Pickett's men had charged. He observed:

> No natural panorama in the world surpasses that which the spectator beholds when, standing on the west of Cemetery Hill, he looks down upon the broad expanse of field, meadow and woodland, dotted with farm houses and barns, the deep red of the newly-turned-up soil in strong contrast with the verdure of growing crops and magnificent groves, and the whole landscape bounded by the outside mountain wall as far as the eye can reach.

It is all still there, waiting for generations to come and see and learn. It will always—must always—remain, to acquaint Americans of all eras with a place that helped make their nation what it is and will continue to be. Gettysburg will be a special place within us for as long as we continue to reach into our hearts to find out who we are as a people.

Most of all, simple ground like the Wheatfield was ennobled by men's deeds.

Published by KC Publications • Box 94558 • Las Vegas, NV 89193-4558

Inside Back Cover: They came and fought and died, and their courageous acts are enshrined forever.

Back Cover: At Gettysburg memorials reach across the ages to the future.

Created, Designed and Published in the U.S.A.
Printed by Dong-A Printing and Publishing, Seoul, Korea